Lost Love

Sandy Lee Carlson, Editor

Orenaug Mountain Publishing

Lost Love, edited by Sandy Lee Carlson

Copyright ©2025 by Orenaug Mountain Publishing

All rights reserved by the poets whose works are in this anthology. No part of the contents of this book may be reproduced or transmitted in any form or by any means, including recording or by any information storage and retrieval system, without written permission from the authors.

Email: hello@orenaugmountainpublishing.com
Website: www.orenaugmountainpublishing.com

Cover Art: Watercolor by Viola M. Jaynes

First Printing 2025

ISBN: 979-8-9925369-4-2

Printed in the United States

Love (n.)

Old English *lufu* "feeling of love; romantic sexual attraction; affection; friendliness; the love of God; Love as an abstraction or personification," from Proto-Germanic **lubo* (source also of Old High German *liubi* "joy," German *Liebe* "love;" Old Norse, Old Frisian, Dutch *lof*; German *Lob* "praise;" Old Saxon *liof*, Old Frisian *liaf*, Dutch *lief*, Old High German *liob*, German *lieb*, Gothic *liufs* "dear, beloved"). The Germanic words are from PIE root **leubh-* "to care, desire, love."

etymonline.com

When you are sorrowful
look again in your heart,
and you shall see that in truth
you are weeping
for that which
has been your delight.

–Khalil Gibran
from "On Joy and Sorrow"

Table of Contents

Introduction	1
Birth, Death, and Resurrection	7
Death Comes	8
Death Calls My Name	9
Tiny Heart Pendant	11
Remembering When I Wanted What I Have	12
Destiny	14
What's Left	15
Never Again	16
Perseids	17
Fermata	18
Deny	22
Jackson	23
A Note From Downeast*	24
Camber	28
The Truck	30
Playing a Round with Pop	34
The First, After	38
Is Your Head Full of Honey?	39
Here Lies Loss	41
Letters That Never Reached Him	42
After the Funeral	44
Fly Away	45
A Heavenly Farewell	46

When You Have to Say Good-bye	47
A Capturing Love	49
Mourning Hours	50
She Rides With Me	52
Duality of Grief	53
Pieces	55
What Is Love?	57
Lunar	59
Lost Limb	60
The Viewing	61
Before the Harvest	62
Tanka	64
At One With the Sea	65
Another Painting, Not Just	67
Presence	69
Fragments	70
Double Pane	72
Evenings Are Always the Toughest	75
Stillness	77
Never Got Old	79
Is There a Room up There in Heaven?	81
Lament	85
Natalie, 1967	87
You Will Live	90
White	91
All I Need	92

Lost Dreams	94
Last Homecoming	95
This Night I Wake up Dreaming	97
Without Carlene	98
Sole Survivor	99
Dreaming of Fish	100
DLM	102
Hiding Place	103
The Gift	105
Twice Lost Love	106
Eight Years After Susan's Death	108
Breath	109
For Dominika	110
My Buddy	111
This Shoal	113

Introduction

Just when the day comes—when there's a particular missing part that overwhelms you with the feeling that she's gone, forever—there comes another day, and another specifically missing part.

–John Irving, A Prayer for Owen Meany

In the years following the suicide death of my dearest childhood friend, his father gave me a dog-eared, yellowed copy of John Irving's 1989 novel A Prayer for Owen Meany. "This was Craig's," he said. "I read it. I thought you'd enjoy it." Coming from a retired marine and a man of no nonsense, his words were as good as a hug. I thanked him and took the trade paperback, which was thickened from readings and rereadings—and intimidating with its creased spine and mysterious armadillo on the cover. How many times had my friend and his dad read the book? How did they understand it? Would I arrive at the same place and be there with them through this text? In taking the book, I accepted the invitation to be with them in love. I brought the book with me on vacation to my parents' summer home on North Topsail Beach in North Carolina.

There, I befuddled the neighbor, a high-strung and very successful real estate deal maker who was sure summer was about doing things—boating, fishing, drinking—as I spent my days on the front porch of my parents' home reading a novel that unlocked for me a very dear friend as its words tapped out for me the meaning of friendship in a curiously specific New England Morse Code of complex sentences and unashamed directness. The novel—a story of friendship, loss, and unremitting sorrow—broke my heart and healed it like a burl on an oak tree. I read it again and again and took hope and heart in a celebration of oddness unique to New England, where nobody needs you to be there unless, of course, you are and someone local derives value and meaning from your presence. This novel requires a certain amount of sitting, something the neighbor down South did not understand but accepted as he took my daughter out on his boat with his family while I read and found myself at home.

Craig was there as I read. His parents came to Connecticut in the 1970s, when his father was a rising executive for Texaco. They settled in Danbury, where I lived after moving from Bethel with my family when I was six. I am being specific about town names to be clear that I am not from Danbury, where I grew up. I am from Bethel, just a few miles away, where my life began. I was new to Danbury when I entered the second grade, as Craig was when he came there in the fourth grade. We both grew up in a town where the children read different books from the ones we did in our earliest years. Our growing up was shaped by a sense of being from someplace else, of not quite belonging. For both of us, this was a good thing because we stood out, and our teachers recognized us as curious, engaged learners, anomalies. We were the manna that teachers thrive on; we would do what we were told and do it well. We affirmed our teachers' value because the quality of our work was evidence of their effectiveness. For us, school became a place to be safe and to be valued. We found our way in by dint of our hard work driven by a deep need to be accepted. Reading was the route home.

Church was also a place to be safe at a time when church membership amounted to the signing on to the belief that we all have something to offer, and kindness can make a difference. Then, Christianity was not a recipe for rightwing nationalism; it was a path to the bake sale that led to eternal life in heaven. I met Craig when we were in the eighth grade, when we attended confirmation class at the Danbury United Methodist Church, where the Reverend Terry Wayne Pfeiffer was pastor. I was enamored of the tall, funny kid from across town who attended Rogers Park Junior High. During that time, I, who attended Broadview Junior High, looked forward to our weekly classes because they afforded me the opportunity to be in Craig's company. In church, I found a very human, adolescent, visceral hope.

Remembering those weekly lessons on what it means to believe, to have a spirit, and to encounter the Spirit, I recall the afternoon light streaming through the classroom windows and warming our backs as we listened to our loving pastor. Confirmation class was a welcome break from the dreariness and regular brutality of junior high. Even better were the Sundays when Craig and I would acolyte together, carrying into the sanctuary the symbolic light of Christ's love and carrying it out again. I cherished those bright and fleeting moments.

Confirmation class paved the way for friendship in high school, where Craig and I had classes in common. Our friendship grew as we navigated what seemed to be the overlarge, anonymous world of Danbury High School in the early 1980s. That was a time when we were invisible to our teachers as we ground through lectures and worksheets. In junior year, Craig and I had an overweight, unsympathetic algebra 2 teacher who promised to "roll all over" us if we didn't do well on his tests. To this day, I have no idea what that meant—other than some form of an unmerciful humiliation. But those were the 80s, and I can appreciate those years as a time when I learned to be accountable for myself, my learning, and my success. Craig and I understood it as a time, also, to expect no mercy or understanding from the adults around us. Our job was to support each other, and that is what we did.

We lived in a world where you had to figure stuff out. We were the children of Baby Boomers, who also had to figure stuff out. Our parents were the beneficiaries of the largesse following the Allied victory in World War II. Born after the worst deprivations of the Depression and therefore not old enough to serve in the military during World War II, they knew they damn well better show up to work hard and be grateful within the almighty American system. To do less would be a disgrace to those who had gone before and those who struggled silently as they aged beside them.

As they worked hard, President Johnson passed the Great Society legislation that would honor all Americans as deserving of support through hard times as well as deserving of their right to vote. Johnson would make real and measurable the 14th and 15th amendments to the US Constitution. Johnson's groundbreaking legislation would pave the way for a deeper understanding of and respect for what it means to be a human being in the United States. Title IX would follow. Eventually, so would protections for gay Americans—though the Equal Rights Amendment would continue to languish. Even now, women remain the great threat to the Great Society.

Among the many things Craig figured out during the 80s was that he was gay. He made the realization at a time when the world didn't much welcome the discovery, and he kept it to himself until his therapist told him he had to tell his parents. He test-drove the revelation by telling me and then my mother one evening when my dad was working late. I was not surprised or bothered; my dear friend was sharing more information about who he was; so be it. I welcomed the confidence and treasured it as a gift from a dear friend. He told my mother; her earth did not shake, either. She told Craig he was our friend. He asked her if he should tell his parents.

She told him not to; they wouldn't be ready. He took her advice and chose a moment that he coordinated with my family so that he could come to our home if he encountered any resistance or anger at home. We had snacks and a bed ready for him in the event that things did not go well.

When he told his parents, they were surprised, but they told him they loved him. They wanted him home. He came by to let us know that, and we told him the door was open. We ate the ice cream we had bought to cool the heat of family friction. All would be well.

The road ahead for Craig would not be an easy one as he sought acceptance. He wanted to live an honest life; he didn't want to pretend he was somebody other than the gay guy he was. That meant we who knew him should know he was gay. For all of those who accepted him, there were plenty who did not or who put qualifiers on their love or not-so-veiled judgments. There were more "I love you even though you're gay" messages of so-called support than Craig could bear.

Craig was a dear friend to me and my family. He was a pal to my daughter; he was the giver of her first three Margaret Wise Brown board books and her partner in the completion of her many wooden jigsaw puzzles. He loved her, and she knew it in the way of small children and loved him back with her whole, unconditional heart.

But what we had to offer was not enough to convince Craig that life was worth sticking around for. Ultimately, Craig took his life on Good Friday, 2001. Possibly. His mother said the date of his death was either April 8 or April 10. Holy week closed the opened tomb and left us wondering what it means to love and to hope and to start over.

My husband and I spent a lot of time with Craig's parents in the decades following his death, and they became our friends, a second set of parents to us and grandparents to our daughter. We loved them very much. Our relationship grew past our grief and took on a life of its own, though Craig was the nursery tree that gave life to the flourishing forest of our friendship.

In 2018, we would lose Mrs. Lundwall, Petria. Mr. Lundwall, Rich, would pass in 2021. They left behind photo albums and Craig's journal of poetry. Among those albums was the Lundwalls' wedding album and Craig's college photo album. I took them because nobody in Craig's family wanted them. A year after Mr. Lundwall passed, I reached out to family members to ask if they would take these documents, but I received no response.

Today I have Craig's album and Craig's journal. I have the memory of our friendship. I have in my heart the love he held for me, and I for him. I have, also, the hope and sorrow of an empath who would open the floodgates of love to others who have experienced lost opportunities in life to share the love in our hearts.

Lost Loves is an offering from writers around the world who have suffered the loss of a loved one. We have put words on our love to honor those who have passed and to honor those whom we love here and now.

Sandy Lee Carlson, Editor
Orenaug Mountain Publishing

Birth, Death, and Resurrection

By Craig Allen Lundwall, Danbury, Connecticut, United States

Joyful now, the rivers of my eyes have run dry
Light now, at last the coal black tempest has passed,
Free now, the chains of pain are severed, my soul emancipated
Relieved now, I exhale, dispensing my fear of the future
Hopeful now, my spirit again free to imagine, able to dream
Awake now, part of the Circle again, I spin new sensations
Rested now, vitality regained, I engage all I see
Peaceful now, the Meaning revealed,
I have mastered the lesson.

Death Comes

By Terez Peipins, New York, United States

Death comes,
the end of the
waterfall
where drops
rejoin
and form the soul
that floats.
This earth
missing you
turns tears
into words,
words
Into honey.

Death Calls My Name
By Faith Vicinanza, Southbury, Connecticut

Half-dreaming, I hear my name, more echo
than spoken, as if a query on the tongue, his,
followed by a slight pause prompting a reply.

Were it your voice, I'd come in flannel, barefoot,
from this pretense of sleep. Days bulk up,
become weeks, weeks becoming months
that gather a chill in the linings of their coats

and should they find me alone at night
wandering directionless, they will be ready
to beckon with the promise of shelter
in their wintry arms—with a promise of sleep

where I might hear your voice whisper my name.

A call comes

for you. In a rush, I tell the voice on the other end
what I daily tell myself cannot be true. I keep busy,

avoid talking about you with friends. I have taken
to drinking wine. I have taken to working long hours.

I have taken to not opening the mail. There is never
much of interest and no one to share it. I have taken

to staying home. The camera has stopped working,
your car won't start, a construction crew guts

your old office because the septic tank failed
and flooded the finished basement. Each day,

it's something more—old wiring, old plumbing,
no insulation in two exterior walls, leaks formally

hidden behind sheetrock. This house cannot stop
its hemorrhaging as if in sympathy, and I want

to do the same, heave up this despair, this sorrow,
this missing you, until I am emptied—

lie down on worn deck planks, warm in the sun,
sleep—dream of you.

Tiny Heart Pendant

By Amanda "Rory" Meyer, Illinois, United States

i still remember the first time
you thought i was my mother,
all those years ago
in a suburban, midwestern mall.

so much of our overlapped adult lives
revolved around your illness,
and a part of me wonders
if you had been able to remember me,

would you have been proud of who
i became? would you have enjoyed
the times we spent together the way i did?
these days, i am scared to wear my tiny heart

pendant that contains all i have left of you.
it's not really all i have left—you live on
in my memories, but memories are fleeting,
and i am terrified that mine will betray me too.

and how could a world possibly carry on
where all that's left of your love and your light
and your stories and your wisdom
is hidden inside a tiny heart pendant on a chain?

Remembering When I Wanted What I Have

By Mary Moody Hunt, Ohio, United States

A leaky roof, uneven floors, no bathroom sink.
Boards on the porch rotted in the rain and sun,
well water iron made white clothes orange.
and that God-awful fake paneling everywhere.

I longed for a green metal roof, kitchen cabinets,
outlets that didn't spark and blow a fuse,
sheetrock walls that I would paint ocean blue,
a bathroom with vanity and glossy white sink.

Raised three sons, worked hard,
educated and self-educated, climbed rungs.
One evening, when I was exhausted, hubby
cooked a western omelet and fed it to me.

He clipped my toenails, brushed my hair, applied
lotion, cuddled with me through movies, cooked
my favorite meals, made me feel as though
I was the most beautiful woman in the world.

I wanted a porch with white wicker and cushions,
living room drapes not purchased at Family Dollar,
a cozy fireplace, matching dinner plates,
a lighted bathroom mirror to apply my make-up.

We built the dream, painted walls, put glass fronts
on upper cabinets, tiled floors, bought drapes and
dishes, decorated the porch. First visitors included
pancreatic cancer and the grim reaper.

During full moons I stand at my bedroom window,
stare at the old house crumbling out back, memories
like chimney smoke float through the air and I
ache for the days when we had absolutely nothing.

Destiny

By Shelly Rodrigue, Louisiana, United States

It was always my destiny to lose you—
from that first glance in high school halls,
I looked into your eyes and knew

nothing lasts forever—it's true
a heart shatters when it falls
as was always my destiny; to lose you

a pang no narcotic could subdue
yet I would risk the void's endless walls
because looking into your eyes I knew

in your own way you loved me, too
content I was to be your thrall
and was always; my destiny to lose you

bred fear in me and wild it grew
a massive ache, its will to sprawl
until I looked into your eyes anew

that deep, rich brown of a Cajun roux
wrapped around my soul like a shawl—
it was always my destiny to lose you.
I looked into your eyes. I knew.

What's Left
By Catherine Lee, Texas, United States

Some time ago we spent
long years as lovers,
spoke delightedly
of having children once,
our twins.

Facebook stalking decades later
finds you married happily
(what I desired for you)
with doting adult children, in-laws, grandkids,
wishing you good health and godspeed
going toward your 62nd year. That year.

Then someone changed your Facebook moniker,
added RIP.
Not a thing exists of what we were.
No contact with your family I knew,
all gone to spirit, I suppose,
they of years gone by.

For me to even grieve what might remain
long past our discontinued troth,
what's left, has left behind
odd sense, bereft.

Never Again

By Jackie Chou, California, United States

I go to where I last saw you,
where plum blossoms
painted the road white,
to see you again.

But the ground is swept clean
by leaf blowers,
and it is only me
on the grey concrete.

I go to where I once saw you,
where the crescent moon
hung like a metal hook,
to see you again.

But now the moon is full,
and for all these days and weeks,
I have not yet found you again.

You, a passerby
of gardens and night skies,
never to be caught
at the same place again.

Perseids
By Martin Giroux, Connecticut, United States

so i dedicated
my life
to the study
of the perseids
each night
my face
amid stars
reflecting
back at me
in black pools
of cool water

i rubbed my
squinting eyes
to find that
in the multitude
in the division
we become
not many
at all
but one

Fermata

By Joseph A. Farina, Ontario and United States

memory lady
you are not bound
to passing times and yes
it's long been over
but trees and water mirror summer
and that's the time for lovers—
time to sleep
upon the fumes
of some rare watching hours and walk
through empty twilight parks
my arms about a stranger
soft and woven as your body
—a now different shelter—
 there are times
 when men have need
of stranger songs—
they are no different than yourself
except for love and laughter
nights of need
with traps that spring upon our brains
where crickets sing seductive songs
covering the summer lovers lanes—

once I was among their chorus

singing with another
the ritual of hand and breast
did you, too, surrender?
you never answered
and now that spring
has long been over—
these days are signs that prophesy
a changing like kisses given at beginning
an inhalation of two souls
we were like that far too briefly
and besides I was the dreamer

ii

you committed the perfect crime
that none shall know its passing
the victim strangled with a hair
finer than your lashes
wrapped in pages of his writings
and buried with his incomplete passion
did you cry the death of summer poems
that were never captured and rationalize
we were not lovers
only merely loving?

popular songs repeat emotions
I thought that I had written

but they were not mine
were never mine and never will be

have you wondered too, if the music
that you listened ever heard your joy
your pain

iii

philosophizing Cohen
and listening for entrances
can make one forget almost every pain
but I remember more

too late to think new words again
so pure and perfect that I
would never need to write again

too late for every dream except
the delicious pain of daydreams
inspired by twilight commercials
and slow motion lovers, caressing
their bodies with kissing sweet lips
their hair suspended in lovers' easy air
their synthesis working
upon silent lives...anything to break
the monotony of time, the perpetual thinking

of faces on visionary windows
degrading to illegible lines

. . . . . .

June July and August
the falling of slow hours
against an arpeggio of rain

strangers are calling
white breasted and bare
up and down the crying street
heavy with lamplight
empty of prayer

the baptismal evening of wandering
but where lady where?

Deny

By Linette Rabsatt, Virgin Islands

Breast cancer denied you
the opportunity to see
your first great-grandchild
our hearts became more heavy
because in a few years
your grandson died
we pray that he rests with you
even as we think about your journey
it makes our hearts continually cry
because we can no longer speak with you
you were denied the opportunity
to see my children graduate
to encourage them to live their best
toward their goals, remain passionate
although we feel that we were denied
just another day spent with you
God had other plans
for us to see his love through you
although you're gone
and life's not the same
it doesn't mean that we've given up
we may be denied another day with you
but our love for you remains the same

Jackson

By Glenis Moore, Cambridgeshire, United Kingdom

It is 30 years now since we met
that long hot summer school week.
I was listless and looking for the love
I could not find in my mistake of a marriage,
and you? Well, you were always looking.
You flattered me with your attention,
your implied devotion, your passion
and so I thought, wrongly as it seems,
that it would be easy for you to leave
the wife you swore you had never loved
after my partner left me for a mistress
I didn't know he had. But, of course,
you did nothing of the kind. Instead
we spent four years in discrete hotel rooms,
snatched hours of tenderness, which
I always arranged, brief phone calls,
two weekends away and then nothing.
I just stopped calling you. I was
simply tired of your boredom,
your false promises and my despair.
I'm sure you replaced me quickly enough
with your easy charm and barely
thought of me again. But you are
still buried deep within my soul, walled

up there as the man I truly loved
But really shouldn't have.

A Note From Downeast*
By Ronald Hugar, Indiana, United States

I loaded the car and drove overnight
because I wanted the presence of her.
I tried to call, but the lines were down
between Seal Harbor and Plantation Island.
"High seas and foul weather," the operator explained.

(Dear Ron, Just wanted to say hello,)

I booked a room at an inn
on a sand beach in Portland.
The ribs of three tall ships
poked through the surf
like fingers caught
in the act of closing for prayer.
The spray tasted of sweat
and the air of flesh gone electric.
I drank some coffee, read *The Boston Globe*,
and listened to the sea digest yesterday.

(this being a bad time for me)

I drove four more hours without sleeping
in the hope of catching the last ferry of the week
from Bass Harbor to Frenchboro,

but I missed it by a day.
A lobster boat, about half a mile offshore,
explored the edge of a fog that floated
above the ocean's heavy swells
like the breath of a ghostly lover.
The skipper dieseled north by northeast,
against the tide,
then turned about to return
the way he had come.

(very troubling in these heavy fogs so utterly obscuring...)

Twilight kissed the night.
The engine of the lobsterman
fell silent. A light rain began to fall.
The boat drifted.
The tide clutched its sides.
The skipper stood at the gunwale,
hands on his hips,
staring into the pall.

(but time passes, doesn't it?)

Her summons yellows between the pages
of a book I never finished reading.
The fog settles on my shoulders.
The day drifts into gray.

(even though it goes nowhere
but turning in on itself–Arin)

*Postmarked FRENCHBORO, ME; October, 1987

Camber

By Bobby Steve Baker, Arkansas, United States, and Canada

The Cautionary Man wakes in pieces—
momentarily paralyzed
vision frozen on a vision he has dreamt
so dreadfully many times.

Slowly rolling now he feels
the camber of the bed is off.
Nothing has prepared him for this unbalanced bearing
of the bed he slept steady on for years.
Looking over to the other side he blinks and blinks
to clear his eyes and sees
there is no counterbalance—
as if there's no one there.
He reaches over and throws the covers back
and there is no one there.
Struggling mightily to come awake
he walks around the bed to kneel at the other side
stretches his arms across the indentation in the sheets—
and there is no one there

He begins a ritual
to quell this mounting fear
of being overwhelmed by death, by grief.
The Visionary Maid is gone

and will not balance out the kilter of this bed.
Neither can he balance out
the unpaired valence of his heart.
He takes time, slowly breathing out
listens to the deep reptilian brain saying to breathe in.
After a while a bitter lonely voice says
You have dwelt in this reality enough
sleep now and dream unsettling dreams.

The Truck
By Dan Hubbs, New York, United States

He couldn't remember much
At the end of his life,
My dad.
He didn't know who
I was.
He'd wake up
Pointing at nothing.
He asked where
His mother was.
What? my mother said.
She's been dead for years.
No, he said,
Pointing,
She's waiting for me.
He'd mumble,
He'd whisper
Something and
Stare into space.
Well, we're going
To say a prayer now,
My mother said.
Okay, said my dad.
Hail Mary
And so on

Now, and at
The hour of our death,
Amen.
He looked over,
He was holding
My mother's hand,
I don't like that
Last part,
He said.
We all laughed.
We watched his old face
Mouthing no words,
His cloudy eyes,
Bones of
His hands
Pulling on the
Sheets,
Over and over,
Picking at the fabric,
Like pulling weeds,
Faster and faster
Staring at the
Spot by his leg.
You took my truck,
He said.
What? my mother said,
You don't remember!

You were driving all
Over hell and creation.
Lucky you didn't kill
Someone.
You did,
He said,
You took my truck.
I'm doing everything for
You, she told him.
You're not doing anything
For me,
He said.
Yes, she said.
She started crying.
Here, I told him,
We'll get you sitting up
A bit better.
You can watch the
Yankees.
Okay, he said.
I got my hands
Under his arms
And heaved him,
Best I could,
So he was sitting
Up almost straight.
I turned the TV on

And found the ballgame.
He leaned back
Into the pillow
As the Yankees
Came up to bat.
You took it,
He said,
My truck.
You took
My truck.

Playing a Round with Pop
By Michael J. LaFrancis, Windsor, Connecticut, United States

"Family matters most" was his response to the question.

He had a son, then a daughter
then two more sons.
He never knew how she did it,
raising them that is,

into four mature adults,
each with their own successful career,
while still working as a first-grade teacher,
always having a meal on the table.

Almost sixty-five years ago,
this stylish, toy salesman hustled
to the first tee, to meet
a sleek twenty-seven-year-old,

brown-haired beauty, inquiring with a smile:
"Do you want to play a round (the clubhouse)?"
Two years later, he closed the sale.
He made a good choice.

They became friends,
before they became lovers;

playing a round of golf or dealing cards,
going to live theater, traveling
to Bermuda and Florida, before returning
to their dream house on Cape Cod.
They left all their problems,
on the other side of the bridge.

He was always so grateful to have her to love.
Pop knew it was important to get there first,
because "the early bird always gets the worm."
He always planned to be there,

at least ten minutes early, because for him
being on time was a matter of trust.
Pop also found he could catch more
bees with honey than he would with vinegar,

so he managed his game that way. Pop knew
he had to work for the rest of his life,
so he might as well do something
he enjoyed doing. Pop really wanted to

bring comfort and a smile to a child lying
in a hospital bed so he stuffed their gift shops
with plush teddy bears. He knew that being there
at the top of the scoreboard gave him more

control over his schedule and how much
money he made, rather than sitting in an office,
where everyone got the same two percent raise.
Pop grew up mostly under the influence
of his single mom, a champion who played on
after her partner went out of bounds early
in their match. Her country club became
his day care and they became members

of the dawn patrol; he and his brother
learned to be men from many different role models,
and play their next shot from wherever it may lie.
Pop had to hit out the rough after his employer

suddenly went out of business,
though he recovered skillfully
starting one of his own. This time
all his eggs were not in one basket.

Thirty years in sales as a leading money winner
gave him plenty to meet his financial goals.
He paid for three college educations,
one trade school, their retirement nest egg,

and all uninsured health care expenses,
so the family would never have to.
Nearing ninety and ready to putt out,

he wryly added: "There will still be money left
for you kids, if we ever die." These days Pop
is playing extra holes, as his family shares
their favorite Popisms with the five grandchildren.
They can still hear his voice whispering in the wind:

"Don't forget, get married and have lots of children."

The First, After
By Laura DiCaronimo, Massachusetts, United States

What was once comfort is now treachery
minefields I'm forever dancing across,
waiting always for the torrent of tears and snot when I land on something unexpected:
the way tomato paste falls from the can,
old coffee, burned.
It's tradition, so I brace myself. The boxes in casual, predatory wait
lined up from the basement. Changed the Glade to pine already: it's festive.
Rallied to action, my infirm fingers dig through tissue paper.
Caught on old hooks, also the norm when the snow starts falling.
I can't find the angel with my name painted on it. Frantic, scooping lace and wood with equal insouciance. Eyes unfocused on everything but how I remember her loopy penmanship made a capital L.
Footsteps on the basement stairs, he's laden with another box. My legacy in his devout grasp. His body behind mine, voice low when he explains he already put up the things he thought would be hardest for me to cope with.
Grateful again I wrote my suicide notes in pencil, my editor turns them into poetry now.
He shows me where she's sitting on the tree
winged and waiting. Tears blur what I see of his face before he holds me
but I think we're both smiling.

Is Your Head Full of Honey?
By Linda M. Crate, Pennsylvania, United States

i see you in
every bee

once a bumblebee
was buzzing loudly
in my apartment

when i first woke up—

i remember we were
at the nursing home,
you held a book called
forget-me-not like the flowers;

i laughed when you asked
me if i could borrow a billion
dollars—

but despite the fact that you
were mostly yourself,
the dementia set in and you asked
if we left you here to die;

and where did the bees go?

i wonder did you go
where the bees went,
is your heaven full of honey?

Here Lies Loss
By J.M. Summers, Wales, United Kingdom

Here lies loss,
grief presenting itself
in ways that are prosaic.
It is always too late.
To take flight, to realise
that the sun is not kind.
It would be better to
emulate the swallow and
flee the coming season.
But we, lacking the wisdom
evolution has granted,
will remain ice bound, suffer
the cold of winter, and
realise too late that the
remaining time is
always too short.

Letters That Never Reached Him

By Sunila Javaid, Lahore, Pakistan

I wrote him letters
that never really reached
Telling him I miss him
every single day of my life
Does he know?
How would he know
I wrote him letters
that never really reached
He left me at the beginning
when I was to be so close to him
screaming, sobbing,
Couldn't even say the last goodbye
I wrote him letters
that never really reached
He told me he loved me,
held me in his arms.
I crave to be held again
How would he know
I wrote him letters
that never really reached
Five years to this scar
I still cannot move forward
Is an exam so important?
Couldn't even say the last goodbye

I wrote him letters
that never really reached
Everyone thought I don't feel a thing,
oh to be understood
the thought of him torments me
How would he know
I wrote him letters
that never really reached
even his Sheiru has a sheirni now
I'm still caught with my studies—
Couldn't even say the last goodbye
I wrote him letters
that never really reached

After the Funeral
By Katrina Kaye, New Mexico, United States

The enormity of death can be too much at times;
the finality of it, too overwhelming.
Instead of contemplating prayers
or words of solace, the void is filled
with the ordinary.

How important these sweet rituals,
these sweet, sweet rituals of routine
that once seemed so meaningless,
but now hold the only kind of salvation
that can comfort.

Tomorrow we can talk of heaven.
The day after, discuss the roles of death and then
the philosophy of a life well lived. At some point
we can talk about dinner plans and
the obligations of the weekend;
at some point we must be able to compose
a way through all those things left behind,
but for now let there be silence.
but for now, we can remain together,
hands close, but not yet touching,
learning to form words as if for the first time.

Fly Away

By Cendrine Marrouat, Winnipeg, Manitoba, Canada

When shadows dawn upon the world,
And colors start to fade,
Love still remains in the heart.

When heavy rain pours,
And thunder rumbles,
Eyes can still see.

May you find the light,
The guide to your inner steps.
Love never dies,
So do not fret, and depart.

Vanished though you are,
Your memory still endures.
Your soul needs repose.

Now, shadows are upon us
And colors are fading, but
We know we will see you again.

A Heavenly Farewell

By Joseph C. Ogbonna, Nigeria

My dearest departed to the
distant clouds flew.
She was clad in pristine white,
glittering pearls, glamorous and
ebullient roses.
She was ferried by a dozen
cherubs in a celestial cruise,
bound for the idyllic shores
of heaven.
Congratulations my beloved!
You have meritoriously earned
the saviour's kiss and warm
embrace.
Sojourn in bliss, and never cease
our cause to plead before His
majesty divine.
We sure hope to someday share
your infinite joy, when at life's
twilight, we will be ferried in His
Majesty's service, "HMS Life Eternal."
Happy eternal vacation to you, Mum!

When You Have to Say Good-bye
By Sam J. Rabinowitz, Cherry Hill, New Jersey, United States

So many times when I was young
I needed help and you were there
A gentle smile, a tender touch
A soothing hug to show you care

But now you're gone, your time has passed
And still the memories will ever last
It's just so hard to have to say good-bye

As I grew up you made the time
To be with me no matter what
And yet I find I still want more
But now that door's forever shut

And so I grieve for what I've lost
You know I'd pay whatever cost
Just so I would not have to say good-bye

I always knew the day would come when I would face an empty chair
Still as I look out on that space I can't believe that you're not there
The weight that's on my shoulders grows, the sorrow deep within me flows
It hurts so hard to have to say good-bye

When came the day that I was wed

I saw the pride upon your face
As one by one my kids were born
They felt your warm loving embrace

And your capacity for giving showed me how I should be living
I just don't want to have to say good-bye

Then it was time to care for you; it was my turn, I did my best
And though you tried to stay for me, you are now finally at rest
The times we shared, the fun we had
I find I'm smiling though I am sad
The time has come for me to say good-bye

But in my heart and in my soul
You are the part that makes me whole
And while your face no more I'll see
You'll always be the best in me
So as the tears flow down my cheek
I'll stand up tall and loudly speak
That I will never truly say good-bye
No, I will never ever say good-bye

A Capturing Love
By Hanh Chau, San Jose, California

Precious love remains
in memory through the intertwined
soul of the far-distance realm
Lost in the emotional wave
Soft breeze maintains
Bitterness comes into place
Echo of reminiscing embrace
Each heartbreak, it stays in silent
Tears streaming
with deep soul pain
Transcended into despair
that set us apart in this world
Until we meet again
when destiny brings us
back with the rekindling of light
with the promise of time
Like heaven and earth
made for each other
In a boundless and endless
traveling journey
through the guiding star
to be reunited forever

Mourning Hours
By Madlynn Haber, Massachusetts, United States

The dead are as alive to me today as ever.
Their numbers increase in quantity and quality
as each year, more pass on.

Some are known only by a name,
while others were deeply loved.
The loved ones dance in the recesses of my heart.
I could mourn some hours of every day.

Like sunlight on snow, there is a brightness
lighting the days ahead.
It will be an easier drive to the next aunt's funeral
if the weather is clear.

There will be joy in the company of mourners.
Delight in remembrances of celebrations,
years upon years of shared nourishment,
attention, visits, arrivals, and departures.

This aunt gave me a gold rug for my room,
a bandage for my blistered foot,
a place to sleep when I was lost.
She welcomed my baby, celebrated her growth.
She encouraged my care of my mother,

helped me to honor and bury her.
She pulled out the strength I needed
to heal my own illness.

"You'll always be one of my own,"
she said in our final conversation.
She resides with all my own dead now.
I mourn for some hours of every day.

She Rides With Me

By David Bigham, Waterbury, Connecticut, United States

she rides shotgun
in a long distance
waking dream

the glint in her eye
flickers like an
indicator light

her lips are moving but
the words are drowned in RPMs
and Stevie Ray Vaughan

my hand on the wheel
is just a bit
beyond her reach

another streetlight-strobe
stop-motion old movie night
on the freeway

Duality of Grief
By Jeannette Zallar, Texas, United States

You raised me
but you also razed me.

You taught me about God
but you taught me about pain.
You taught me how to balance a checkbook,
but you said no one would ever love me.

Forever unyielding,
Forever abusing,
Forever unending,
A punishment for a crime not mine.

When I got the call at seven a.m.
On a Sunday
from the sibling you loved above me
I heard her scream
"Mom's gone!"

A duality of grief.
I mourned for the child within.
I mourned for the loss of a parent.
I mourned the fact I could not properly mourn.
(Don't speak ill of the dead; don't speak ill of the dead).

Family rushed in,
including my older and my younger siblings.
They wailed, they screamed, they cried.
I, the unfavored one, was silent.

I handled all your affairs; I hope you saw.
Your debts are gone; you can rest in peace now.
I paid for your headstone, along with a friend.
I bring you *ofrendas* as tradition requires.

I hope you saw as the family came and picked everything apart.
Vultures in the skies were kinder than they were.
All I have from you is a CrockPot, and a ceramic bowl
Made in Mexico, it says. It's my favorite one.

One day I'll see you again; for now I live on.
I write little tributes here and there.
No one ever knows, as they like the posts,
the duality of grief.

Pieces

By Ryan Douglas Roth, Alberta, Canada

When he was sure
That she was Her,
Her who had once been,
Her of Her and Him,
And when it was too late
For him to contemplate
Escaping from the past,
For she had seen him pass,
Drowning in his breath,
Resigning to capitulate,
He approached his ex.

"How have you been?" he asked.
"Supreme—and you, since I'd last seen?"
"Well, you could say…"
He choked on the phrase,
While he pined for glory days.
She saw his gaze,
And knew his daze,
But she said, "I cannot stay."
"See you around," she said, and left,
He found his pain renewed.

Although ago, his heart had cleft,

This seeming split today was new.
It hurt this time she left him too—
With wretched waves refreshed he knew,
A heart can break in more than two.

What Is Love?
By Roxanne Berry, Yorkshire, United Kingdom

Love is letting go.
Even when it hurts the most.
When his eyes are no longer bright.
When powerful muscles that carried you across the land in flight are withered and worn.
The truest love lets go.

His voice that chimed with the sunrise and under moonlight is the sound of love.
Never forget it. Let it sing in your ears.
From the first day his warm breath touched your cheek to the last breath he takes.
Be there. Love him.
Love him enough to let him go.

Stroke his neck, once glossy and strong.
Let your fingertips send him comfort, love him more now than you did then.
For he has given you his all.
His heart. His spirit. His love. His life.

Do not abandon him to take this final journey alone.
Your presence will keep him calm.
Your love will give him courage.
Smile and whisper softly in his ears.

Talk to him of happy times, for there have been so many.

The woods you roamed, the jumps you flew, the snacks you shared.
Together.
Tell him you'll love him forever.
His legs are tired now, they tremble when he walks.
Legs you brushed and booted, legs that took you to the stars, further than you ever imagined.
Please be there when they fall, because that is love.
It will break your heart to see it, but it will break his if you are not there.

Love is limitless.
It knows no bounds and cannot be restrained.
Pain is fleeting, though it often feels too long.
Know that love is eternal.

Friends and family may see your joy and sadness, know of your dreams and desires.
But the one you love most of all is the one who shares them with you.
He has been there by your side each and every step of the way.
So be with him when he takes his last.

Don't hold on too long.
When he tells you he is tired.
Listen to him. Trust him.
And when the time is right, love him enough to let him go.

Lunar

By Israel Allen, Tennessee, United States

She is fair-skinned
And easily bruised
Her gentle beauty
Scarred from the abuse

I must be the moon
She talks to in her sleep
Just after she prays
The Lord her soul to keep

When the morning sun rises
She forgets I exist
Or calls for a cloud
If the memories persist

Just two weeks from now
I will find myself new
And she will cry out
For a vision of blue

So I will return
To cast rays on her night
A fool who believes
She'll love me in daylight

Lost Limb

By Nancy Lubarsky, New Jersey, United States

Years ago, winter's tail splintered a huge
branch in our backyard. Through the seasons
we had watched this tree rise toward the sky,
observed how the branches multiplied,

changed wardrobe. My young son noted every
new appendage, saw them all as family. So
this strike was painful. Subsequent storms only
made things worse. The fissure spread, the branch

gradually dropped toward the earth. My son
mourned our decision to remove it that spring. He
wondered if the tree sensed the loss or imagined
that the branch was still there, as people who lose

limbs do. And now, years later, he's divorcing.
No violence, no rage. Just a small fissure that
turned into a larger one. Only this time he is the
one deciding and we are the ones who mourn.

The Viewing
By William Perley, United States

I remember my father's face
like soap or polished stone
His chin and nose seemed larger
His hair was combed in a way
I don't remember
He was wearing a black suit
It fit him perfectly
But I never saw it on him
before
I've seen the tie

What a handsome man
You can see it easily
Even now
They must have seen it too
the ones who painted and pumped
him

There's his right hand
Those were his veins
I remember that hand
I remember when it was huge
and held mine

In memory of my father, Cyril William Perley, 1912-1992

Before the Harvest

By Jim Lewis, California, United States

yes, yes, we all know
you did the disappearing act
took your unique little laugh
and your nearly silent sighs
and the tangibles that made
an unpredictable life
infinitely bearable

but then so much of you stayed
i find your fingerprints
highlighted against the blush
of tomatoes ripe and gathering dust
waiting for your hand to coax them
into waiting baskets

twin hollows greet me by the squash
where you knelt patiently
weeding and watching for the signal
only you could see, a quiet invitation
to an intimate soup or soufflé

purposed footprints, abandoned trowel
carefully positioned hose, wanting only
the turn of the faucet to flow again

everything in this garden a witness
to your deep reluctance to leave
before the final harvest.

Tanka
By Maria Tosti, Italy

elsewhere opens up—
among ethereal shades
the moon rises
on your white robe
the melody of the wind

At One With the Sea
By Marianne Tefft, Toronto, Ontario, Canada

My father was at one with the sea
In his arms the water was my best friend
When he carried me into the waves
I body-surfed timelessly lips blue
As if I had fallen through northern ice
Into subtropical winter
In his youth he was jettisoned
From the deck of a warship
Into wine-red seas
With nothing of Greek poetry about him
Only his self-inflated jeans and swollen belief
In the rightness of his cause and his Almighty
To carry him through six days afloat
Beyond the range of the Japanese guns
Seven nights clinging to sharp sand
In chest-deep water close to shore
For what could a Connecticut Yankee know
Of the nocturnal habits of sharks
Perhaps the fear of drowning or worse
Already had been wrung from him
By the swinging vine from which they uncoiled him
As he hung head-down in the mill pond behind the barn
Where he began a lifetime of horse-whispering
He saw the light that so many claim to have seen

And because I believed my father to tell the truth
That I seldom have trusted from others
I learned never to fear death
To let salt spray and Moon rhythms
Spur my stroke through my terrestrial nights
Even into submarine days
Where my bullish head told my marathon heart
It's only four kilometers and no one need imagine
You've fallen from a cruise ship
Even if the current carries you down
And the islands seem to repel one another
When you are in the middle of the channel
Many Decembers before I carried my five-day-old child
Into the indoor pool of our lakeside apartment
She keeps a later photo of my father
And her a blonde toddler in a life vest
Helping hand on the pool skimmer
When she remembers her Poppy
She recalls the sting of chlorine
And the abiding comfort of learning to swim
From the lip of his pool into his sunlit embrace
It pleases me beyond all reason to know
That she knows what I know
My father was at one with the sea

Another Painting, Not Just

By John R.C. Potter, Turkey

Another Painting...

1.   her beloved granddaughter was ill. she was cradling Jo Ann in her arms, the rocking chair keeping in time with each heartbeat. creaking, clacking, cosseting. trying to keep the fever at bay with her love. the baby's mother had been in the hospital for months due to depression after her daughter was born. then Jo Ann pointed at the old, time-worn painting on the wall above the sofa: at a mother with her young children in a rustic cottage from yesteryear, perhaps from the country of their forbearers. there was a swaddling babe in a cradle on the floor. together, the two of them looked at the painting that hung there in pride of place. two generations separated them, these two females—one near the end of her life, the other at the start of hers—but viewing the painting as one.

Not Just...

2.   after her husband passed away, the grandmother went into a rapid yet long decline. what had been thought to be grief and loss that addled her mind eventually ended up being diagnosed as dementia. her house and furnishings were sold. she was placed in an old people's home behind locked doors. when one of the woman's daughters took down the old oil painting from its permanent place above the sofa, she found an inscription on the back. "This is Jo Ann's picture. from Grandma."

Not Just Another Painting...

3.   tick, tock; click, clock. decades passed by in the blink of an eye. flowing, fluttering, flickering. that child grew up, married and became a mother with a baby girl. the river of life churned on. a few months after her 65th birthday, the woman who had been that baby girl passed away suddenly, her heart giving up the ghost of its host. she fell only a short distance from that painting that hung in its pride of place above her sofa.

This oil painting is in the author's family; the painter is unknown.

Presence
By Jacek Wilkos, Poland

I'm lying on the beach.
The July sun hides behind the horizon.
No soul in sight,
I'm surrounded by nature,
untouched by human hands.

Memories come back alive.

The sea whispers my name with your voice,
the wind strokes my face with your kisses,
warm sand reminds me of your cuddled body,
the stars shine with the glow of your eyes.

It almost feels like you're here with me.
I fall asleep with a smile.

But at some moment
the wind will stop,
the sea will calm,
the sand will cool,
the stars will hide behind the clouds.

When the sun rises
and the sunlight wakes me up,
I will still be alone.
At the beach and in my life.

Fragments

By Donna Langevin, Ontario, Canada

I miss my poet's glass pencil jar
engraved with a plume and my name.
After you borrowed and broke it,
it left shards in my heart.

Today as I visit a potter's house
built from broken ceramics,
I picture you restoring these walls
after your seizures chipped your coffee cups
and smashed our wedding gift platter.

I mourn my glazed horses with lost legs and tails
after your elbow grazed them
and they leapt from the windowsill.

As I edge down the hall of this pottery house, I recall
the hand-painted plate you hurled
after you found my lover's letter.

Wondering why we lingered in our shattered marriage—

Was it your porcelain promise to quit drinking
or the sunbeam that lumined the seams
of a clay goblet you mended?

Maybe it was the hours you spent
trying to glue my bone-china horses
and your love that helped repair me
when I fractured my pelvis at the bus stop.

For Richard, d. 2018

Double Pane
By Bonnie Morrissey, Vermont, United States

I was so yours, opening
to touch under the covers
of that October sky in Vermont.

You were so mine, lighting up
like the farmhouse windows
blinkering on in the darkness.

Double pane, to keep out
the winter chill, I told you
as we embraced. On a scale

of one to ten, we fell through
and landed in a pile of leaves,
laughing in every color. We were

turning magenta and then
we were crimson. Together
in a season of death, we watched

the thing that was indestructible
not die. A single stem in an antique
vase, like the Buddha himself

on the dining room table,
having left this world in lotus
position, body refusing to decompose.

That flower wouldn't die, but we were
caught in the downward spiral
of the season, thousands

of orange and yellow bodies
sailing towards earth, madly
fluttering or rising for an instant

To the gentle touch of air,
arching their backs to the sky
one last time, a vestige of free

flight before landing in a mosaic
of nostril-flaring musk. We kicked
that dank smell up, we fell down again

in them, we burned sage, but your lips
thinned and our sweet, sad, short-lived
life together was over. We fought

destiny, we were turning
inside out, we were burning up,
and our smoke sent a tribute

to the empty treetops. I took you
to the airport. Double pane, I mouthed,
as your plane sailed west across the dark sky.

Evenings Are Always the Toughest
By Nancy Manning, New Haven County, Connecticut, United States

Summer mornings I await your letter,
watch the carrier pass by tanned,

empty-handed.   She frowns,
I feign a smile. Inside my room

I sink my head

              on my pillow—

wait

for tears

      over the bond you broke. Back

in May, we sat on the shore
of the campus pond,

held hands, promised hearts.
Now
    evenings alone, I ponder

on my porch what was supposed to be.

The crickets chirp,

the fireflies flicker one, two, three.
I retire into the night.

Darkness
                    cradles me. My heart aches
        as I poke and prod the ashes

            of
            your
                Words.

Stillness

By Cheryl A. Rice, Ulster County, New York, United States

In stillness, when all else fails,
gnats circling fluorescent lights
like cartoon stars,
I know you worked night jobs,
bus station security,
pandemic silence, even gators
gone into remission.
I hope you saw a glimpse
of what is beautiful in Florida,
beyond the highways, strip malls,
beyond overdeveloped condos
blocking the bay, beaches gated off.
There are stars everywhere,
when sand glitters under our New York feet,
when the sun rises quick and hard
over the flat tropic horizon.

There is a blot for me now,
where your sun declined,
that makes me see all thru shit-colored glasses.
The imperfections are in focus now,
as much as the magic castle in the distance.
I see the wires guiding Hook's grand galleon,
and the man behind Chewbacca's mask.

Only Dorothy remains true,
pining in a Kansas cornfield for rain and shoes.
I must remind her that the story
doesn't end with the first book.
I hold your unread chapters gingerly,
then remember we all have
our own books.
We live our own tales,
dying sometimes by the sword,
sometimes by starlight.

Never Got Old

By Edward Dzitko, Southbury, Connecticut, United States

"I'll know I'm getting old,"
the father said,
"when you beat me."
The son dribbled the ball
atop the key.

They stood there in the street,
hoop at the curb
in front of the small house,
just enough light catching
the rim and net.

Barely twenty years apart,
They played often,
after dinner nights,
after chores on weekends.
The games were all.

K, old man, the son thought,
juking left, then,
hard step and drive right.
The father's hand shot out,
to steal the ball.

Seven straight makes later,

and game once more.
Beating the dad, turns out,
Required much more work.
The dude had game.

He had earned a free ride
To college
in the 60s, but in one
final high school quarter,
that dream ended.

Scholarships vanished
When cartilage tore.
Recovery as unclear
As a cancer fight'd be
in his 50s.

The son graduated high
school and college,
married, and the street games
became some casual,
easy shootarounds.

Father died and his son,
in the casket
put a ball for next time.
"Never beat you, Pop, and
you never got old."

Is There a Room up There in Heaven?
By Prithvijeet Sinha, Lucknow, India

Is there a room
up there in heaven?

Or are there
boughs
holding still
to your kite
in a windless world?

Is there really
a room up there
in heaven?
Or is it open for admission
somewhere
close to a city
named Ambrosia?

***

Hissing lawns prevail—
where the sprinklers
satiate a thirst
for knowledge
regarding earthly

fortunes
and every element—
from worms
to herons,
star-shaped leaves
and the elegant trinity
of brown, green and tangerine
indents—
has the dream-like quality
you nurtured,
like Pegasus
resting under the same boughs-
holding still
to your kite.

***

In my world,
there are open rooms
without a bed.
The eyes
become catacombs
under false ceilings.
The light comes!
Tears from heaven
roll around
sometimes like bitter honey

on spring's little fingers.

***

In my world,
the acoustic refrain
leaves no desire
to keep
that stool
by the piano
in the studio.

That warm, enveloping
cloud
that is a man's voice
is like New York,
a state of mind,
a nameless city
saving its last bells,
distracted and yawning
at the window
that opens up
to the ether.

My world
grieves.
The song is like

a boy
who went with the child
lodged in his chest
and became a cloud.

A poem inspired by Eric Clapton's immortal "Tears In Heaven"

Lament

By Karen J. Ciosek, Connecticut, United States

If I could have seen you then,
one more time,
I wouldn't have let you go.
I would've wrapped myself around you,
linked my arms into yours,
discussed the war,
my starting college,
your junior year.

I would have pressed closer to you
to listen to you breathe,
to sense the heat of your body,
to melt in the sound of your voice,
your laughter,
smile.

I would have felt safe
in your hands,
my heart opening to yours,
knowing our differences,
culture, religion
didn't matter.

Your caring for me

shone in your eyes.
You must have seen
the same in mine. But

fear from my father's
glare of disapproval
held me back then...

when you and I
could have been "us."

Natalie, 1967

By Susan Marie Powers, Connecticut, United States

I

By the expanse of Lake Maxinkuckee,
on train tracks ringing the water,
we stretched our legs to reach tie after tie,
avoiding sharp white rocks between boards.
Two boys ripped by on their father's motorboat,
weaving wildly close to us, shredding water lilies,
spraying a silver plume.
They hooted to our young figures,
but we were busy singing "Cherish."
We'd spent nights in your room
watching the small black disk spin.
Our voices lurched as we hit the ties hard,
tried to land squarely in the middle of each.
Next to me your tanned skin glowed
against a white tee, and tight, yellow shorts
hugged your legs, your knees cinching
the full curves of muscles.

At thirteen, womanly hillocks coursed your body
into an astonishing silhouette, while I hung
slender and shapeless, marveling.
We called ourselves twins, alike only in

height, hair color, and a love of laughter,
the warm intimacy of girls become step-sisters,
girls who had found live-in best friends.
I envied your flat belly and high breasts,
not knowing someday
an abortion would strip away the only life
ever to grow in your womb.
Not knowing I would never bear a child,
no matter how hard I tried.
We were young listening to the record trill,
"You don't know how many times I wished that I could hold you."

II

The large blue lake, the smell of marshy decay,
the sharp odor of gasoline,
somewhere the scent of honeysuckle.
Children curled into cannonballs
and hurled themselves off piers.
My eyes are blue, yours were brown,
your even white teeth broke the surface
of your lips. High cheekbones and ears
like halved apricots.
That day we walked and sang,
I did not hear the distant whistle of the train
until I shouted, "Get off the tracks,"
only to find you frozen, your eyes fixed

on the large white eye of the train bearing down,
no one but me to stop your death—
"Move!" I shouted, but you stood
transfixed by the looming metal
of machinery. And so I moved instead,
grabbing your arm, pushing you.
We fell together down the hill.
A rolling tangle, sharp stones cutting into our hands crying,
"What happened? What happened?"
"Cherish is the word," still echoing in the hot summer air.

Twenty years later you took
your husband's gun from his police car,
pressed that dark metal against your high forehead.
And I who lived a thousand miles away
cried to the sky: "Natalie,
didn't you know I would come?"
I would have pulled you off the track,
rocked you as that train screamed into
the blood-splashed sunset.
I would have cherished you.

From Break the Spell, *published by the New London Librarium (2010)*

You Will Live
By Martina Rimbaldo, Krk, Croatia

Remembering the past where simple imagining of your future passing would force my eyes to be filled up with sorrowful tears.
I wonder to myself how I managed to survive that unpleasant but inevitable event, given that for me there was not enough time to process your loss of life. Writing this text with one year gap I wonder if I was being egoistic thinking more of me not you… All I may hope for that you are in a better place. If not, I will pray night and day for your soul until it finds the peace. I promise, you will forever live through me, as long as I walk, as long as I talk, you will as well live.

White

By Irina Tall, Poznań, Poland

White on white
White...
Everywhere, as if...
In the eyes, in the fingers, in the auricle...
White on white,
In the hands, in the nails
Glare on the glass,
On the shoes,
In the interweaving of skyscrapers,
In the reflection of faces in the mirrors,
In a bucket of foam, a cleaner on the fiftieth floor,
Inside a flower in the thicket,
White,
And I want to bite
Marzipan, becoming sweet on the tongue, melts, white...
I know that it envelops me
Like a cloud, white on white,
I'm riding in an elevator with white buttons
Similar to pills,
White...
a man takes my hand,
But I don't remember him...
and his hair
White as milk...

All I Need

By Steve Walter, Kent, United Kingdom

If I were to be honest all I need is what I am.
So why do I long for her, her taste, her touch

Her sex? Surely knowing that I could…
Ought to know to be enough. But I do not want

Only to remember her warmth, her kiss,
Her skin, her smile, her playful laughter.

What I want is to relive those first few weeks,
Months, hours, days, when there was nothing

In the world that mattered more
Than to be together. When our embrace

Broke the hearts of lovers not yet born
And we took what we each had to give

As if it were a child, to grow with us.
All I need is what I am. I am that child in her.

She is in me. I cannot forget. I even remember
The shapes of the bedclothes each morning

As if our every movement were captured
In their soft folds, mounds and crevices.

And I remember the voice of the singer
Who sang to the bonding of our muscles

And limbs, matching the rhythm, and sang again
The day we parted, releasing each other.

Lost Dreams

By Norma Zimmerman, Massachusetts, United States

I knew,
the moment you were conceived,
deep within my womb
safe, secure, secret, silent

There you grew,
and I felt you dance
to the beat of your heart,

in a purple leotard,
pink tulle skirt
ballet slippers.

Spinning on one foot,
arms above you wide, waving,
your dark hair swinging around
your face,
laughing like you could dance forever.

Then I felt you fall,
collapsed legs,
still arms.

The beat of your heart was gone.
All my love couldn't save you.

Last Homecoming
By Peter Newall, Odessa, Ukraine

Evening. The valley
dumb,
the autumn sky clouded,
its flat cloth
pierced by silent birds.

Those days
when the sky rang blue, like copper,
will not come again. Nor
the eager green growth
of new plantings. Only
what is already known, known
too well, the marked
wooden table, the candle, the door
barred at night.

And nor will sleep come, that sleep
put aside joyfully at morning; only
a dusty quiet, the eyelids dry.

We came here first
in youth. Then
the mornings were long, fresh, the afternoons
slumbrous, sunlight slanting

through the windows, golden. And every night
a half moon, high, silver; we
were rich. We knew nothing
of time.

But time knew of us. And counted us,
folded us in, then divided us.

Now I alone breast the hill
to look down
on the empty house.
Just once more to enter, find
the kettle, make up
the bed.
I have no need
to bar the door this time.

This Night I Wake up Dreaming
By Judith Liebmann, Branford, Connecticut, United States

In deepest sleep I find myself alone
strolling in a landscape so familiar
I must dream it up night after night:

I walk unrushed along a cliff-edge path
above a beach where sanderlings
scurry after ebbing waves—back and forth,
looking for stirred up isopods to eat.

The path descends, along a stretch of dunes
where sedge grass grows in tufts, down to
water's edge. There are seashells strewn about
and drying strands of washed up seaweed.

At this place where land meets water
will you be there, waiting? Will we
linger side-by-side, our feet washed
by the waves, sinking into dampened sand
that anchors us forever to that spot?

Even in my dream, before I wake,
I know I will not find you waiting. Even there
your presence wanes, beyond illusion or recall.
How is it I can dream a landscape so precise
and comforting and real, yet I cannot conjure you.

Without Carlene

By Sherri Bedingfield, West Hartford, Connecticut, United States

Walking toward the river, once, I followed a woman. She had dark hair and reminded me of my long-passed cousin. I always wanted her to be my sister.

In yellow grass, by the walk, a flock of grackles chattered and grazed. Someone was fishing at the short river-dock. That day two older women under wide-brimmed sun hats shared a bucket of minnows for bait.

Carlene and I, if we stood side-by-side, would never look like sisters. Carlene, dark-haired with hazel eyes and me, a pale, skinny, blond girl. She, like me, didn't have a sister.

She worked in her husband's office with two other women. Her husband slept with all of them. She never got over that. There must have been other things, other reasons. She shot herself in their backyard next to a blooming azalea bush.

When I walk, especially in April, I walk with Carlene. I like to forget that she's gone. I imagine I'll see her at the next corner. At Martha's, the luncheonette on Main Street, we'll get our sandwiches and old-fashioned Coca-Colas.

Sole Survivor

By Samuel Gluck, Connecticut, United States

There is a disruption in the field
Something is not the same
There is a crack in the ground
A blow in my mind
A tear in my soul
A rip in my gut
A bleed in my heart
I am shocked and stunned
Something has drastically changed
I am confused
Reality has been bent out of shape
and will never be the same
She is gone
They are all gone
Only the fading wake of the memories
Of what once was a life a love a family
And I alone am the sole survivor
The final repository of all that once was
The joys and the pains
The love and all its stains
The first born and the last
to cherish and keep all of what used to be

Dreaming of Fish
By Tom Nicotera, Connecticut, United States

When I think of you I recall
the early morning ride to West Hill Pond,
car hugging curves,
sun just rising,
lake surface shimmering,
air vibrating with the fish to be taken,
the giant trout lurking,
perhaps even the rare and fierce
landlocked salmon.

$2 for a boat gave us the day afloat
and after donuts at the dockside grille
we spent the day skimming the water,
the line tugging at our hands,
spinners dragging down the minnows
to the numb-cold waters where trout stirred.

The sun's quiet heat was broken midday
by a feast of grinders and cold sodas
and whatever talk mulled between us.

We stayed till we caught our limit,
five trout each which Mom would clean that night,
then fry the rich freshness

in egg and milk batter.

We stayed till sometimes one,
sometimes four, whenever that limit came.
But we stayed together,
man and boy,
poles held taut,
boat gently rocking,
swallows skimming the surface,
clouds floating in water,
waiting for fish,
dreaming of fish.

For my father

DLM

By Davion Moore, Ohio, United States

A dear friend
A mentor
A hero
All of the above
And more
My grandfather
A man with the kindest heart
Selfless
Inspirational
A pillar
Brilliant
A star
Who shined
Everywhere he went
You are
Forever in my heart
Forever in my memories
And I will
Carry on the legacy

Hiding Place

By Bryan Franco, Maine, United States

It has been too many years since we last saw each other.

We were still in love when life threw multiple wrenches at us.
All we could do was duck and cover and run
or risk permanent injury.
There was too much that
was beyond our control.
We knew we'd never be
the same again.

After we ended,
there were times I wished
my love for you had been unrequited.

Just under three years later,
you introduced me to him.
He insisted I come to the wedding.
He even sat me next to his redheaded friend
at the singles table as an obvious set up.
The wedding was the last time we saw each other.

I was genuinely happy for both of you
after your child was born.
I mourned our potential child

we used to talk about all those years ago.
You wanted a boy named Sylvester
so we could call him Sly.
I wanted a girl named Mazzy named
after my grandmother Mazel Tov.
You said you'd think about it.

You had a way of humoring me
as if your veiled validations were hugs
made of homemade hot chocolate
and melty marshmallows.

Once, when I was in town visiting my mom,
your mom called and took me to lunch.
She said she always wished that we
had made it through the trouble.
She proceeded to show me
photos of her grandchild.

Your husband called to invite me to the funeral.
He said that you valued our friendship and
wished we hadn't fallen out of touch.
My heart aches that I wasn't able to be there
for your mom or him or to say goodbye.

You will always be the one that got away but
stayed hidden deep in my heart until the end.

The Gift
By Viola M. Jaynes, Texas, United States

I didn't count on losing you
To the shafts of steely flames.
I didn't count on losing you
To the claws of depression's drain.
I didn't count on losing you,
To untruthful screams within your head.
I didn't count on losing you,
To dark corners of isolation's threat.
I didn't count on losing you,
To such distorted and unimaginable pain.

Twisted contortions have mangled
My internal solid frame.
A shattered heart, a shattered soul—
Is now a gift wrapped in unidentifiable,
Distorted and unimaginable pain.

Through a dimly lit veil, I know
Your atoms and your energy are alive.
Expanding, exploring—with uncompromised eyes.
I am learning to perceive you anew—with such tenderness,
This is my truest gift—recognizable
And wrapped in unimaginable Joy.

Twice Lost Love

By Isabell VanMerlin, Sonoma, California, United States

He was so tall
    6'4"
Kinda geeky
overbite
cowlick
drove a yellow Scout
The Lemon.
I was smitten.
I thought he was, too—
we got pinned
on the third date.

His family, all the boys, were engineers.
He was different;
    majored in Philosophy.
I was an Art major—and Spanish—
    just back from my junior year in Seville.
He was a sophomore, I was a senior; we were the same age.
We both smoked; we both liked to drink beer.
We only dated on Saturday nights—both of us studying hard.

I made my best grades that semester…
But somewhere along the line, after Christmas,
    I discovered…

      he felt guilty;
      he had been innocent.
I couldn't change who I was
    nor the experiences I'd had
    and he couldn't forgive himself.
I was devastated—and I had to end it.

He went on to do really good things
    a humanitarian
even worked through the government
    doing good things.

I never forgot him.
Years later, in a moment of nostalgia,
I found his obituary online.
He died after a fall down stairs
    to his *pied-a-terre* in DC.

I felt like I'd lost him twice.

Eight Years After Susan's Death
By Adair Heitmann

Tuning fork for veins
Your untimely death remains
How to calibrate?

Candle flame snuffed out
Sucker-punched by your demise
Empty and nauseous

Tears swell in my eyes
Why then did you have to die?
Your spark doused too soon

How to carry on?
With so much of you now gone
Memories don't help

Your laugh, your strut, you
That's all I want, only you
Memories won't do

Breath

By Cheryl Panosian, Connecticut, United States

A chill comes over the skin
knowing I can't watch his breath again,
knowing his chest won't rise again,
but lay flat,
a body of skin and bones.

They take the body and discard it
before an attachment to an empty shell occurs,
but the memory, the memory
of his cool skin haunts the day,
haunts the night
haunts the breath I hold
between my lips.

I breathe now as if I could
blow life into him.

To comfort us they say God has taken him.
Who is this god that steals breath
thief-like in early morning hours
just as night has given way to dawn?

In church we light candles, hope
his breath will fuel the flames.

For Dominika
By Michał Mazurkiewicz, Poland

Your look,
in dreams and in sleepless reality.
Like a few notes in a tune once heard,
stubbornly stuck in my head.
Like a poem
woven from the drops of this spring rain
that never stops falling.
Like your secret.
Your one word
and the colours of meanings change.
Even hurt is bearable.
Wasted feelings
do no harm.
They're like flowers on the grave of dreams.

My Buddy
By Katherine Baker, Connecticut, United States

to me,
your life was a gentle
spring breeze
blowing by and
caressing my face
like the sweetest
black raspberry hidden
behind the brush

this morning
when I woke
just as soon as consciousness
drained into me
i pictured you
running through
the grass,
golden boy

every moment
with you was
a sweet dream

the pleasure
of knowing you,

i will keep
close in mind
until we meet
again and again and again

This Shoal

By Sandy Lee Carlson, Connecticut, United States

Through the summer haze filming the skyline,
I saw you in the mighty cumulus clouds
Rising from invisible volcanos
Just below the glassy sea's surface
As if you had come to say there is more
Above, below, beyond what you behold.
We are here. Our souls, at sea, are home.
Let your heart remember: Open the door
To eternity. Remember and live.
The granite sands hold the heat of memory
Of spirits, living. Lapping water listens.
The sky and sun feel the press of your breath.
Every life is a keeper of Earth soul.
Open your heart. Stay, a part of this shoal.

About Orenaug Mountain Publishing

We believe that poetry has the power to create community, connect us to each other through our experiences, and place us in communion with our world.

We are committed to publishing poetry that is both challenging and accessible and to giving voice to those who might not have previously had the opportunity to share their work with a wider audience.

Orenaug Mountain Publishing produces themed anthologies throughout the year by poets answering the call and from the work of those poets published in the Orenaug Mountain Poetry Journal, an e-zine that publishes the work of emerging and established poets.

Orenaug Mountain is a 78.45-acre town park located in Woodbury, Connecticut. The park is situated on a basalt (trap rock) ridge overlooking the Pomperaug River Valley. The main entrance to Orenaug Park is flanked by two stone columns with stones that have been cultivated from all 50 states. The mountain is named after the Orenaug people who once lived in the area. The tribe's name means "place of the great rocks." The mountain is known for its dramatic rock formations and natural amphitheater.

Other Books by Orenaug Mountain Publishing

Brand New Season (2025)

Muse (2025) by Samuel Gluck

I Know Myself as Thief (2025) by Jo-Ann Iannotti, OP

Personal Freedom (2025)

Alpacas in Green Pastures (2024) by Caroline Cornelissen

Instances of Seeing, Volume 2 (2024)
a collaboration with Flanders Nature Center (Woodbury, Connecticut)

We Are Here (2024)

The Nature of Woodbury (2024)

a collaboration with Woodbury Public Library (Connecticut)

Whose Spirits Touch (2024)

Winter Glimmerings (2024)

From Art to Art (2023)

a collaboration with Woodbury Public Library (Connecticut)
Instances of Seeing (2023)
a collaboration with Flanders Nature Center (Woodbury, Connecticut)

The Harvest and the Reaping (2023)

www.ingramcontent.com/pod-product-compliance
Lightning Source LLC
Chambersburg PA
CBHW080545090426
42734CB00016B/3206